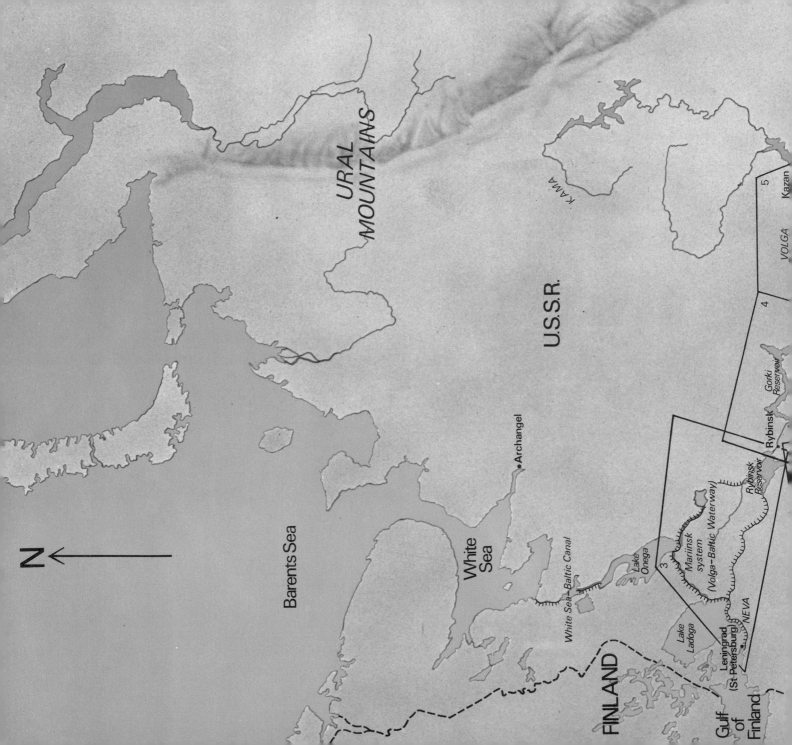

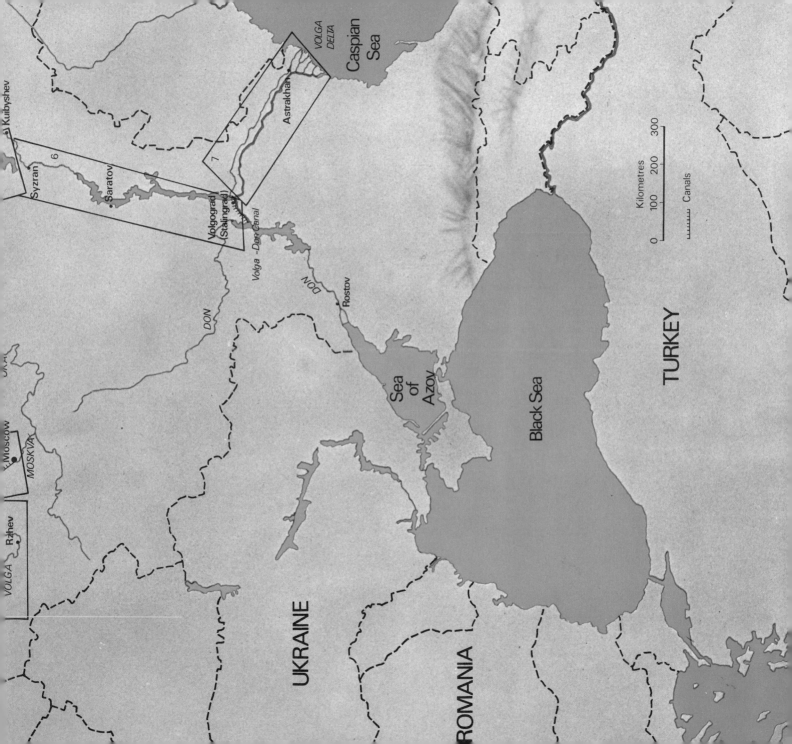

VOLGA DELTA

Caspian Sea

Kuibyshev

6

Syzran

Saratov

7

Astrakhan

Volgograd (Stalingrad)

Volga – Don Canal

DON

DON

Rostov

Sea of Azov

Black Sea

TURKEY

UKRAINE

ROMANIA

Moscow

MOSKVA

Rzhev

VOLGA

Kilometres

0 100 200 300

Canals

Author

Jane Werner Watson has travelled widely throughout the world, and has spent time in many parts of the Soviet Union. She has combined a career as writer and part-time teacher with a deep interest in the people and cultures of various nations. Aided by her own firsthand experience, Mrs Watson has written over two hundred books for children and given a number of lectures on countries in both Europe and Asia.

Series Consultant

Dr E. B. Worthington is a consultant ecologist with a particular interest in hydrology. He was President of the Committee on Water Research of the International Council of Scientific Unions.

The Volga

'Mother Volga' is the most famous of all Russia's rivers:
every part of its long and winding course is connected
with the history of the Russian people, and today it is still
the main street of their vast country. The Volga has now
been linked with a system of rivers, streams and reservoirs
to form a waterway which opens up the heartland of
Russia to several seas, providing the nation's main route
for both internal and external trade. The dams within this
system produce much of the power for Russian industries.

In this book we look at the influence of the Volga both
past and present, and the way in which man has
controlled and utilized the river's resources. The author
also shows us the beauty of the Volga and its landscapes,
and the ever-changing way of life of the people who live
along its banks.

The Volga

Jane Werner Watson

Wayland/Silver Burdett

Rivers of the World

Amazon
Colorado
Congo
Danube
Ganges
Mississippi
Nile
Rhine
St Lawrence
Thames
Volga
Yellow River

First published in 1980 by
Wayland Publishers Limited
49 Lansdowne Place, Hove
East Sussex BN3 1HF England
ISBN 0 85340 750 9

Published in the United States by
Silver Burdett Company
Morristown, New Jersey
1980 printing
ISBN 0 382 06373 2

Printed in Italy by
G. Canale & C.S.p.A., Turin

Contents

Introduction: a network of water highways

The Volga, Europe's longest river, loops through the wide Russian plain for about 3,680 km (nearly 2,300 miles). It follows a roundabout course from marshy springs in the low hills of the north-west all the way to the Caspian Sea.

The Volga's fame does not rest on its length, though. Nor does it depend on dramatic scenery, for the river boasts no mountains, gorges or foaming waterfalls. In fact, all along its course it falls in level no more than 230 m (750 feet).

The Volga is the main artery in a vast network of waterways. Together these streams lace the relatively flat land — forest, grassland and finally, in the south, semi-desert — that makes up European Russia. Along its course the Volga is joined by no less than 200 tributaries, and an estimated 150,000 streams and rivulets. Although many of these are small, some carry more water and flow with more force than Mother Volga herself. It is also interesting to note that about 60 per cent of the Volga's water is provided by the melting of the heavy winter snows of the northern lands. Summer rains add about 10 per cent, and the rest seeps up from underground through springs.

Together, the rivers of the Volga system provide about 32,000 km (20,000 miles) of water highway. This route is heavily used by rafts, barges, tugs, steamers and small pleasure craft, for the Volga system carries much of Russia's inland freight and

Above *Sleek modern hovercrafts provide comfortable passenger travel along many stretches of the Volga*

Right *Many tiny streams lace the marshy land in the river's upper reaches*

In old Russia, as today, people carried their goods to markets in towns along the river

half of its riverborne passenger traffic. Use of the rivers in terms of freight-distance travelled is still increasing.

Before the coming of railways in the mid-nineteenth century, the rivers were all-important. The old kingdom of Muscovy — later known as Russia — had no seaports, which meant that the country and its people were largely cut off from the outside world for several centuries. Since the country was also lacking in roads, almost all its trade had to

be carried by river. Travel was by river, too: on barges during the summer, and on sledges drawn by three-horse teams called *troika* during the long, icebound winter.

River travel was not easy. The northern reaches of the Volga are usually frozen for more than half the year, and even the channels of the southern delta are clogged with ice for about three months. During the spring thaw, flood waters used to race downstream, thick with plunging, crashing blocks of ice. In the late summer the waters were shallow and flowed sluggishly, dropping silt that formed shifting sandbars and made navigation difficult.

Still, the river highways and byways did provide relatively easy communication across thousands of miles. The combination of this river system and the flat land with no natural barriers, was largely responsible for the fact that the nation that developed here became the largest in Europe. And the heartland of that nation lies within the Volga basin.

Rivers were important to the people of the region long before the dream of a Russian nation was born. When the earliest Slav tribesmen moved slowly into the country from the east, they followed the rivers and settled in small clusters close to their banks.

The first traders to visit these Slavic villages made their way up the Volga river from their settlements in the south. They belonged to wandering tribes who had drifted westward from Asia as early as the third century AD. Amongst these people were the Khazars: they came north in search of goods to sell to caravans from China, for one branch of the ancient Silk Road from eastern Asia to the Mediterranean Sea ran past the Volga delta at the Caspian Sea. The Khazars found a ready market among the caravans for fur pelts of the wolf, bear and fox, and the silky warm marten, ermine and sable found in the northern forests.

Above right *Today railways have taken over much of the river's traffic*

Below right *Bears from the northern forests provided pelts for the early fur trade*

The first governments in those forests were established by the Vikings — the Slavs called them Varangians — who sailed across the Baltic Sea in the eighth century. After landing on the coast, they pushed upstream by boat as far as the marshy coastal streams would support their shallow-water craft. Then, carrying their boats on their shoulders, they made their way through the forests to nearby streams that flowed inland.

With prosperity from the fur trade, and orderly government introduced by the Vikings, the Slavic villages grew into sturdy fortified towns above the river banks. The towns, built around wooden fortresses or *kremlin,* became the centres of city-states. The rulers of Muscovy, one of these states, gradually reached out until its princes became, as they put it, 'tsars of all the Russias'.

In a sense, even the name of the country came from the rivers. The Viking boatmen who first explored much of the Volga system, and other rivers as well, were known as *Rus,* probably from an old Scandinavian word for rowers. This name gradually came to be applied to the whole broad land watered by the Volga and its sister streams.

Before Russia was unified, other foreigners travelled up the Volga in pursuit of the wealth of those early trading cities. Most important of these were the warlike horsemen of central Asia known as

Above left   *Rurik the Oarsman was one of the first Viking invaders of Russia*

Below left   *The Mongol warriors formed one of the best-organized armies in history*

Travellers along the river often fell victim to robbers, who were punished harshly when caught

the Mongols, under the leadership of Genghis Khan.

The Mongols first conquered the cities at the mouths of the Volga, and set up their capital there. Then, in the year 1237, they turned northwards. On their sturdy ponies they travelled swiftly through the southern grasslands, but when they reached the thick, roadless northern forests their progress was slowed.

Then came the winter cold. The Volga froze, forming a wide, ice-smooth highway to the heart of the country. Up this path the Mongols raced, conquering and destroying. And for more than three hundred years the lands along the Volga lay under the power of Mongol khans — or Tatars as they came to be called in Russia.

Since that time the Volga has seen many armies come and go. The river has carried the palatial barges of royalty, gilded and hung with rich brocades. It has echoed to the mournful chants of the *burlaki,* teams of boatmen and women who dragged heavy barges upstream against the current. And along the river banks, on the estates of wealthy families, millions of serfs once lived out lives of hopeless drudgery.

Above   *Kineshma, one of the many cargo ports along the Volga*

Left   *Villagers gather at one of the many small ferry docks along the river*

Uprising, repression, revolution, invasion and resistance — the Volga has been a silent witness to them all. The river has never taken sides in human struggles, but it has not remained unchanged by the activities of mankind. Its channels have been dredged to free shipping from the menace of shoals and sandbars. Its flow has been dammed to soften the force of spring floods and to provide more even depth through the late summer months. Power stations built in conjunction with these dams have put the river to work generating electricity for cities and factories. Water has been lifted up to irrigate wide fields. Canals have been dug to link the Volga system, through other rivers, with distant seas. And through it all the mighty Volga still flows on, pumping, it may well be said, the life blood of a far-flung nation.

From marshy lakes and woodlands

In terms of geological time, which measures ages in tens of millions of years, the Volga is a very young river indeed. Its basin was shaped by the glaciers of the last Ice Age, which retreated northwards only about 12,000 years ago. As the huge ice mass melted, it left behind a wide, gently rolling plain dotted with lakes — the Volga basin — and at its western edge a low plateau known as the Valdai Hills.

The largest body of water on the Valdai plateau is Lake Seliger. Simple hotels and cottages along the lake's wooded shoreline house Soviet workers on holiday, who go boating and fishing. But few of them take note of the small chapel in a nearby marsh. This chapel was built years ago to mark the location of a spring that is honoured as the true source of the Volga.

A number of small rivulets wander through the marshy woods and meadows, and it is not until they join forces that the Volga really becomes a river. The young stream travels on through several wide, low-banked ponds before it reaches Lake Volga, just

Right *A small wooden chapel honours the tiny spring which is the source of the Volga*

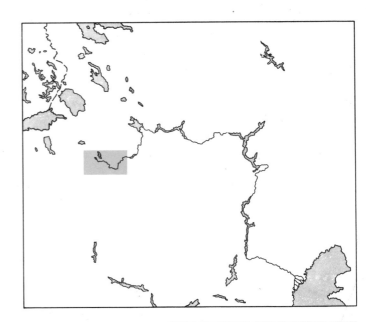

The low-lying upper basin of the Volga is dotted with reedy lakes

Left *Otters can be seen along parts of the river when the water meadows flood*

Below *The government now protects traditionally carved window frames such as these*

Below *Serfs in a village on the banks of the Volga in the nineteenth century*

beyond which it encounters the first of many dams. This is an old dam, but it has enough control over the flow to make the river barely navigable upstream. A traveller wishing to venture on to the Volga here would need a raft or a small, flat-bottomed boat.

The Volga is still a modest, shallow stream as it continues its long journey towards the south-east. Through the centuries it has cut a terraced trench into a hollow in the Valdai Hills, and here it is joined by a tributary coming in from the south, which deepens its flow. Small villages of wooden houses with carved window frames look down upon the stream. Ducks and geese bob on the waters; cows graze on grassy banks. Women come down to wash their laundry in the running water. Pigs forage in the

Above left   *Harvesting cabbages on a collective farm*

Above right   *Many villagers grow flowers, fruit and vegetables in their own gardens, and sell them in the city markets*

colourful gardens. In these homes, the way of life has changed little for several hundred years.

Villages like these once belonged to vast estates owned by noble families, and country folk were tied to the land as serfs. Now most of the farmland belongs to either a collective farm or a State farm. On a collective, or *kolkhoz,* workers share in the profits made from their crops. On a State farm, or *sovkhoz,* they are paid wages.

However, most country people prefer to work in their own small garden plots. Potatoes, cabbages, carrots, cucumbers and fresh greens from these gardens fetch good prices in city markets, as do cherries, apples and other fruits from their trees. Pigs, chickens and cows owned by these families also provide much of the meat for city and town dwellers.

The first notable town on the Volga is Rzhev. It spans the river about 160 km (100 miles) downstream from the source, where the Volga starts to leave the wooded hills behind for a wider plain. Rzhev was founded in the eleventh century, when the city-states were beginning to grow up along the river. It was fought over by various princes in those days, and even as recently as the Second World War

17

Horse-drawn carts are still used as a form of transport in some areas

it saw warfare again. Today, however, Rzhev is a quiet town, ranging along both banks of the river. It boasts some factories which attract young people from the countryside, and it has markets to which villagers bring their farm produce. Some still travel by horse-drawn carts, which are well suited to the often muddy and deeply rutted country roads. But more commonly today they ride in crowded buses, with their produce packed at the back.

Not many miles below Rzhev, the thrust of low hills bordering the Volga's valley turns the river sharply towards the north-east. And after flowing for more than 200 km (125 miles) among low-lying fields and small villages, the growing river passes through its first real city, Kalinin.

Kalinin today numbers its people in hundreds of thousands, and the smoke of many factories — producing textiles, leather goods and machinery — drifts out over the river. Kalinin is a typical modern Russian city, with row upon row of apartment blocks in the Soviet style. Before 1932, the old fortified city on this site was called Tver. Several hundred years ago, when Russia was still ruled by the Tatar khans, Tver was the capital of a princedom that rivalled Moscow in power. Its present name honours Mikhail Ivanovich Kalinin, who was born in the area and rose from peasant stock to become president of the Union of Soviet Socialist Republics.

A village in the old princedom of Tver (now called Kalinin)

Moscow

Moscow is located on the Moskva, a minor river which is now linked to the Volga system from a point on the river below Kalinin. Moscow was founded in the twelfth century, and the wooden *kremlin* built at that time was the centre around which Moscow grew. It became an important town, with a trading settlement to the north-east, but was twice sacked by the Tatars in the late thirteenth century. As the town grew, its buildings continued to be built of wood for some time, because timber from the surrounding forests was plentiful.

Under Ivan I in the fourteenth century, the principality of Vladimir was combined with that of Muscovy and Ivan moved his chief residence to Moscow. He now controlled a vital middle stretch of the Volga as well as large sections of land along its upper basin. During Ivan's rule, Moscow increased in area and its appearance changed. The *kremlin* was enlarged and its fortifications extended. Stone walls and churches began to replace the earlier wooden structures.

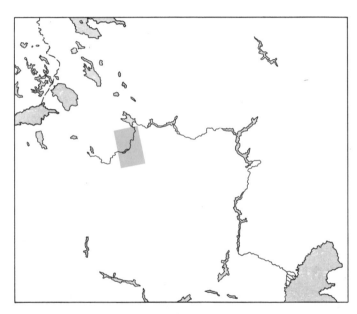

Right *A model of the old summer palace in Moscow. The first buildings were all made of wood*

Modern Moscow is a city of skyscrapers

In the eighteenth century St Petersburg (now Leningrad) replaced Moscow as the capital of Russia

Moscow continued to increase in importance, and became the cultural centre of the Russian nation. It remained the capital until early in the eighteenth century, when Peter the Great built the city of St Petersburg (now known as Leningrad) in the north. After this, the importance of Moscow declined, and although it remained the cultural centre it was little more than a provincial city for the next two hundred years.

It was not until the Russian revolution in 1917, when the last tsar was toppled from power, that Moscow again became the political capital. The government of the newly established nation of Soviet Russia made the tsars' palaces in the Kremlin into public museums. The large open paved area along one side of the Kremlin's wall, known as Red Square, became the site for official processions and public gatherings.

The choice of Moscow as the nation's capital had several advantages. The city is located in the very heart of European Russia, and it lies within the Volga basin which is home to more than a quarter of the nation's people and an even larger percentage of its industry. The surrounding areas contain much fertile farmland: its villages provide grain, fruits, vegetables, milk and butter for the growing population. Railways run out of Moscow in all directions. But until recently the city was badly located for access to the vital river traffic on the Volga. Both the Moskva river and the Oka into which it flows were so shallow that only small barges could use them.

In the early 1930s, the Soviet government set to work to solve this problem. Engineers noted that the Volga flowed past Moscow about 130 km (80 miles) to the north, beyond a range of low, lake-dotted hills. They planned to create a canal system that would join several of those lakes and form a water route between the Moskva and the Volga. The lakes helped by cutting the number of miles of canal that had to be dug; but the hills posed a special

Right *The Young Pioneers' March in Red Square*

problem, for the country between the two rivers was higher than either river. As water does not flow uphill, it would not fill the upper locks in the natural way and so pumps had to be installed.

By 1937 the canal, with pumps and eight sets of locks, had been completed. The system also included several dams with hydro-electric power plants to provide electricity for the capital city and surrounding towns.

One of the dams built across the Volga at this point forms a large lake known as the Volga reservoir. In summer the lake is encircled by green woods and grassy banks. Passengers on large boats bound for Moscow find themselves surrounded by rowboats and small motor boats, for many city families head for the countryside on their free days. Some of them may own or share a small cottage called a *dacha,* and a boat they keep in a marina on the shore of the lake.

Leaving the lake, Moscow-bound boats enter the canal and move southwards through quiet countryside almost to the heart of the capital. There they find themselves in the hubbub of a busy inland port. Large barges, loaded with heavy raw materials for factories and bulky goods for the city's markets, edge up to crowded docks. Tall cranes creak as they dip and rise, loading and unloading. Sleek hydrofoils speed past, almost airborne. And overhead tower the skyscrapers of modern Moscow.

Above *Boating on the lakes in and around Moscow is a favourite pastime for the city's inhabitants*

Below *A boat approaches the imposing entrance to the Moscow-Volga canal*

Left *Crops grown in the fertile farmlands around the Volga are sold in the huge central market in Moscow*

25

Waterway to the west

The canals between Moscow and the Volga were not the first to be constructed in Russia. In fact, that task was relatively simple in comparison with the first canal project that was undertaken — to link the Volga with the Baltic Sea.

It was Peter the Great who, early in the eighteenth century, envisaged such a canal. Before his time, Russia's only seaport was at Archangel, a small settlement at the head of a gulf in the White Sea. The port was so close to the Arctic Circle that it was blocked by ice for six to nine months of the year. But in spite of the difficulties, Archangel's large harbour was crowded during the summer months with sailing ships from Europe. Peter realized that profits from this lively traffic, mainly in timber and furs, went largely to western Europe rather than Russia. He became convinced of the need for a port on the Baltic Sea.

In the course of a long and bitter war with Sweden, Peter, in 1703, at last won his way to the Baltic, or at least to an eastward-poking finger of it. There he

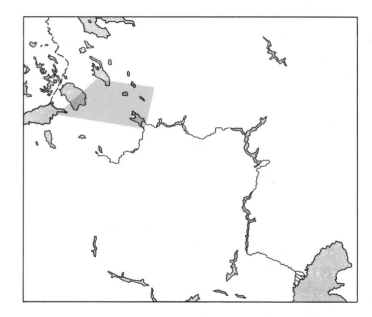

Right *Peter the Great carving a ship's rudder. His fascination with ships and shipping began at an early age*

*Timber from the forests lining Russia's rivers has traditionally formed
a large percentage of traffic along the Volga*

built a fortress, and laid plans for a port city nearby, on marshy islands at the mouth of the River Neva. This was to be his 'window on Europe'.

By 1712 the city — named St Petersburg in honour of the ruler — was complete, and Peter moved his capital there. The noble families followed, and soon countless fine palaces in the European style lined the many canals cut through the swampy delta of the Neva.

But Peter was not content. He needed to link his new capital city not only with Europe but also with the heartland of Russia. Since river travel was the rule in old Russia, he planned to provide this link by means of a canal.

A search of the countryside revealed a possible site. About 160 km (100 miles) east of St Petersburg, two streams flowed about 15 km (10 miles) apart. One flowed westwards to the Baltic by way of Lake Ladoga and the Neva, and the other flowed towards the Volga. Peter determined to connect them.

The building of this Tikhvin Canal, named after a nearby town, through damp and dreary swamp land, was very difficult. The result was rather disappointing: only a few small barges loaded lightly with furs could make their way along the narrow, shallow, mud-banked waterway. Peter the Great did not live to improve the canal, but his efforts laid the foundation for a great project to come.

The next step was the construction of the Mariinsk canal system. This was a 1,215 km (760 mile) chain

Left *This oak tree was planted by Peter the Great during the building of St Petersburg*

of navigable rivers, lakes and canals which was to lead from the Baltic Sea through central Russia to the Volga. The Mariinsk, which took its name from one of its several canal links, was not a very effective waterway either. Most of the streams were so narrow that only small barges could use them. Passage through the locks was slow, and for several months of the year traffic had to be carried on sledges. During the ice-free months, the depth of the water fluctuated wildly. The trip from the upper Volga to the Baltic took, at best, about fifty days.

Still, the journey could be made. Pelts of sable, marten, wolf, and fox from the northern forests reached Baltic ports for shipment to market. Paintings, books, elegant clothing and furniture from European markets were delivered to the estates that lined the Volga and its sister streams.

Above   *The tsar's winter palace, overlooking the river Neva*

Below   *Sable and other valuable furs were able to be shipped to markets once the Volga-Baltic waterway was opened*

Since the wealthy and powerful families were satisfied, little was done under the tsars to improve the Baltic-Volga waterway. But the 1917 revolution brought a new group of leaders into power, officials who were more intent on developing industry than importing luxuries. One of their early concerns was the building of dams, complete with hydro-electric power plants, and the development of waterways.

A dam was soon under construction at Rybinsk on the upper Volga. When it was completed in 1941, the Rybinsk dam was the largest man-made lake in the world, flooding an area of about 4,500 sq km (1,760 sq miles). Tree-shaded river banks, villages and farms vanished under the spreading waters of the reservoir, so vast that it is often called the Sea of Rybinsk.

On the bank of the Volga where it flows out of the reservoir lies the town of Shcherbakov. Completion of this first great link in the modern Leningrad-Volga waterway made Shcherbakov an important port city. Shipyards have grown up along the river banks, and many large barges and other river craft are now built there. Docks poke into the river, and cranes lift goods coming from the Baltic to river boats for the journey downriver. Other goods are trans-shipped there, bound for Baltic ports.

In the old days, barges travelling upstream on the Volga system had no motors to combat the tug of the

Left *The vast reservoirs of the Volga spread across areas which were once rolling meadows and farmland*

current. Until steam power became common in the nineteenth century, boats were pulled by the ragged men and women called *burlaki*: a trader could hire a hundred of these poor people for less than horses would cost him. Roped together, the 'Volga boatmen' plodded wearily up muddy towpaths, dragging barges loaded with heavy blocks of salt or sacks of grain.

Today the *burlaki* have been replaced by self-propelled barges or others which are towed by powerful, snub-nosed tugs. The Volga-Baltic canal system is a busy, modern waterway. The double- or triple-decked passenger steamers, gleaming with fresh white paint and polished brass, often have to wait their turn at the locks. For barges heaped high with lumber from the northern forests, or loaded with factory supplies, are the backbone of traffic on this vital canal.

Self-propelled barges carrying timber (above) *or grain began to replace the back-breaking labour of the burlaki* (below) *in the nineteenth century*

To the Oka, queen of central Russia

Boats leave the Rybinsk reservoir through the diversion channels of its great dam. Now river passengers find themselves travelling south-eastwards, through a narrow tree-lined valley between two low ranges of hills. The boats move downstream past towns, villages and farmland until they reach the next large river port, Yaroslav.

Yaroslav, perched on a high bank above the river, is a city of more than 300,000 people. At its centre can still be seen the white towers of some of the splendid churches built hundreds of years ago, when the town was becoming one of the important trading centres of the north. The skill of the Yaroslav stone-masons was famous, and many churches elsewhere in Russia were designed and constructed by them.

Today long blocks of apartments provide housing for most of Yaroslav's people, as is true in most Russian cities. Downstream, the tall cranes of a busy river harbour angle towards the sky. And at the river bank, within the city itself, a floating ferry dock rises and falls with the changing height of the water.

The rising and falling of the Volga has always been

Right *A village on the banks of the Volga near Yaroslav*

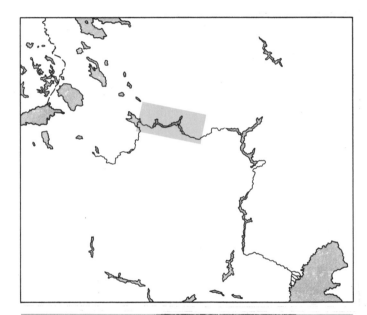

Many churches along the river, such as this one in Yaroslav, had basement store-rooms where merchants could keep their goods

a problem. In the days of the tsars, when the ice on the upper Volga broke up in mid-April after five frozen months, the river in spring flood used to rise 15 m (about 45 feet). It climbed the river banks, eating away at the mud walls. It spread out over the countryside and often destroyed loading docks in its roaring course. But by the end of summer, with little rain, the river would dwindle to a shallow, sluggish stream.

Today the chain of dams along the Volga helps to regulate its flow. During the melting season, these dams hold back much of the flood water in their vast reservoirs. Later in summer they release the water as it is needed. But there is still enough variation in the depth of the water to make floating docks, such as the one at Yaroslav, a practical solution.

Below Yaroslav, as the river widens dramatically, boats chug and sail on what appears to be a broad lake with deeply indented shorelines. The Volga has entered another huge reservoir, which stretches 400 km (250 miles) behind the dam at Kostroma. The water held back by this dam produces 400,000 kw of electricity.

Some say that the modern Volga, with its many hydro-electric dams, has become a series of lakes strung like huge beads on a chain, rather than a smoothly flowing river. Behind these dams — most of which have been built in the twentieth century under Soviet rule — the waters have piled up and spread out. Vast areas of land have been submerged,

Left *A typical row of apartment blocks in Yaroslav*

Above *The floating ferry office at Yaroslav*

Below *Here the Volga broadens out as it enters the vast reservoir behind the dam at Kostroma*

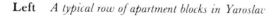

Above *The market and lower town of Nizhni Novgorod in the nineteenth century*

Below *Local craftsmen carved colourful woodwork which was sold at the market*

and whole villages have had to be abandoned and their people moved elsewhere as the waters advanced. But there have also been gains. The remaining farms are protected from much of the spring flooding and summer drought that used to plague them, and those near the rivers now have some irrigation water available. The hydro-electric plants produce electricity to light towns and cities and power the machinery of countless new factories.

The dam is located a short distance upstream from the industrial city of Gorki, where the Volga is joined by one of its main tributaries, the Oka. Gorki was originally known as Nizhni (New) Novgorod, and for centuries its position at the junction of the two rivers made it an important trading centre. Traders and country people travelled long distances by river barge or horse-drawn cart to the city's famous annual fair, when rows of wooden stands would crowd the open squares. Bales and bundles were opened to reveal furs, silks, silver and spices from Siberia, Turkestan and the Orient. Displayed nearby were farm tools, boxes, baskets, gloves, scarves and sacred paintings made by skilled craftsmen from villages in the area.

In 1932 Nizhni Novgorod was renamed Gorki, in honour of Maxim Gorki, a famous Russian author who was born there. Today it is the sixth-largest city in the Soviet Union. Many of the local crafts have disappeared, and in their place are bustling, smoke-wreathed manufacturing plants which produce many of the nation's cars, aeroplanes and military goods. Men and women whose grandparents lived in small wooden houses along country lanes choked

Ploughing a field near Gorki

with mud and snow now make their homes in city apartments. Children have schooling which would not have been dreamed of under the tsars, while their parents work in factories and hospitals, on docks or railways. For Gorki is a major railway centre as well as a river port.

By the time the Oka river joins the Volga at Gorki, its waters have travelled more than 1,500 km (about 950 miles) through rolling hills, fields, forests and marshland. The junction marks the end of the upper Volga, although marshy woodland continues to border the river for some distance as it sweeps eastwards. Towns and cities thicken along its banks. But ahead, as the Volga nears Kazan, a great change awaits it.

Maxim Gorki

37

The middle Volga and the mighty Kama

River passengers leaning on steamer rails now notice that the hilly banks of the Volga are receding into misty distance. The river is entering another of the great 'beads' on its 3,680 km long (2,300 miles) chain: the immense Kuibyshev reservoir.

The Kuibyshev dam, far downstream, was completed in 1957, after which the waters behind it spread out to cover nearly 6,000 sq km (about 2,300 sq miles). The force of this huge reserve of water — released gradually through power stations — produces about 2,300,000 kw of electricity for cities from Kazan to Kuibyshev.

Kazan, with its hilltop fortress, its onion-domed churches, its towers and smoke-stacks rising above busy river docks, is the northernmost city along the banks of this reservoir. Before the building of the dam downstream, Kazan faced the smaller river Kazanka, several kilometres from the Volga. Only in the season of spring floods did the Volga spread to the city walls.

Kazan played an important role in the history of Russia, for its position gave it control over the trade on the middle section of the Volga. The present city was founded by Tatars, and it remained their capital for many years until Ivan IV (better known as Ivan the Terrible) captured it in his drive to unify Russia and to control the whole length of the Volga. Today Kazan is still the capital of the Tatar Autonomous

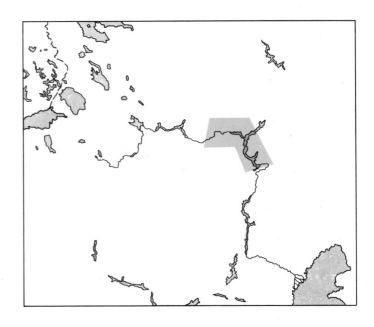

Right *The waterfront at Kazan*

Above   *Kazan is a busy port*

Left   *The armies of Ivan the Terrible won Kazan from the Tatars in the sixteenth century*

Soviet Socialist Republic, and is home to thousands of Tatars who learn their own language in local schools and keep their old culture alive in theatres and newspapers.

The waterfront at Kazan is that of a typical Soviet city. Cranes rise above modern concrete piers where barges are loaded and unloaded. Swift hydrofoils skim the surface of the river, carrying passengers swiftly to and from Gorki. And during the summer, large motorships toot a welcome to the crowds of holiday-makers queueing up for a river cruise. For each year the stretch of the Volga between Kazan and Volgograd provides thousands of Soviet workers with a pleasant week-long holiday.

Above *Deep in the **taiga** forests, through which the Kama river flows before joining the Volga*

Right *River cruises are popular along this stretch of the river*

About 65 km (40 miles) below Kazan, the Volga is joined by the Kama river, its largest tributary. At this junction, the Kama is actually greater in size than Mother Volga herself. It is a mighty river that has flowed down the western slopes of the Ural Mountains in the north-east, and through stretches

Above *The timber rafts which travelled down the Volga became colourful floating homes*

Left *Lenin was born at Simbirsk (now called Ulianovsk) on the Volga in 1870*

of the vast Russian forests known as the *taiga*. Those forests are the source of much of Russia's timber. Logs cut in the northern woods are hauled or floated to a nearby stream. When they reach shallow stretches of the upper Kama, the logs are gathered into huge rafts. Rivermen set up small huts in the centre of these rafts, and their wives move in with children, clothes chests, pots and pans, and often a few chickens. Then they float down most of the 1,600 navigable kilometres (1,000 miles) of the river. Before the dams on the Kama are reached, the rafts are generally broken up. The timber is loaded on to large barges for the rest of its journey, and the raft families make their way back to the north.

Passengers who board a Volga motorship at Kazan have a journey of 130 km (80 miles) before their vessel ties up at the next port city. The port of Ulianovsk stands on a hill above a narrow section of the Volga which is spanned by the longest bridge in the Soviet Union. Ulianovsk is not as old as many of the cities on the upper Volga, but it is a favourite stop for Russian tourists because of its Lenin memorial. The city was known as Simbirsk until 1924, the year of the death of Nikolai Lenin, father of the Russian Revolution. 'Lenin' was the name he had taken as a revolutionary fighter, but his family name was in fact Ulianov and after his death the city was renamed in his honour. His home is now a museum, and a great statue of him stands on a hill overlooking the Volga.

Leaving Ulianovsk, the boat makes its way along the crowded channel. There are blunt-nosed tugs towing trains of freight-carriers loaded with tractors, cars and agricultural machinery from factory cities upstream. Oil-bearing tankers from the distant south steam under the span of the great bridge. And

Above right *A vast modern memorial to Lenin overlooks the Volga at Ulianovsk*

Below right *Lenin's former home has been turned into a museum*

Above *The city port of Kuibyshev*

Left *Wheat flows into the holds of huge barges for transport along the river*

barges loaded with live fish in tanks, vegetables, melons and fruits come into dock to have their loads transferred to railway cars.

Most perishable goods travel by river for relatively short distances, since modern Russia is criss-crossed with railway lines that offer faster transport. But for

The vast car factory at Togliatti is powered by hydro-electricity from the Kuibyshev dam

bulky, heavy loads such as grain and timber, which make up 25 per cent of the freight on the Volga system, speed is usually not important. So barges piled high with grain sacks and logs steam slowly along for great distances.

Downstream, on the eastern shore, the new city of Togliatti, built up around a huge car factory, is still spreading rapidly across the flat countryside. Its location was chosen to take advantage of power from the nearby Kuibyshev dam. River traffic has to bypass the dam to reach the port of Kuibyshev.

This is the most dramatic section of the river. The city itself — the most easterly on the Volga — is low-lying. But across the river the bank rises in towering cliffs, past which the stream cuts its way as it circles in the great Samara Bend.

Through the steppes to Volgograd

With the looping of the Samara Bend, the last of the woodlands have been left behind. Now fields and low grasslands stretch away from the river on both sides, although off to the west the long range of the Volga hills can often be glimpsed.

This mild-looking stretch of the river was a dangerous one for travellers three or four centuries

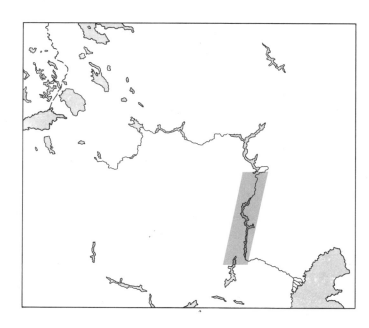

ago. The southern grasslands or *steppes,* which stretch across the country for many miles, were the hide-out and rallying place for the Cossacks. Large numbers of serfs, tired of being bound to estates, fled and joined these bands of roving horsemen in the

Left *The fierce Cossacks once controlled a large section of the steppe country around the lower Volga*

The Motherland figure in Volgograd is the world's tallest statue, and can be seen from a great distance

Above *Stenka Razin was one of the most feared pirates along the lower section of the river during the seventeenth century*

Below *Making tea out on the steppes. The traditional **yurt** tent is still used by the nomadic people of the region*

grasslands. And from their camps they ventured out as river pirates to prey on passing merchant ships.

Today the area is settled and law-abiding. Towns and cities appear out of the mist at intervals. First, at the point where the river turns sharply southwards again after making its giant bend, comes Syzran. Here river traffic passes under a railway bridge, and many of the grain barges transfer their cargo to rails at Syzran's riverside docks.

The next sizeable town is Balkova. Here the Volga, strengthened by still more small tributaries, again widens to the proportions of a lake. The dam which created this reservoir lies far away downstream, at Volgograd. The flatness of the land here has caused the water to spread out widely, but it is rather shallow and many shifting sandbars make navigation hazardous.

Further on, at Saratov, smoke rises from iron foundries, sawmills and railway shops. The town is a busy one, for this is the heart of the true *steppe* country and Saratov has traditionally been a centre for industry and trade based on agriculture in the region.

The giant dam at Volgograd stretches between low banks, and is several kilometres long. Its vast hydro-electric plant has a total capacity of more than 2.5 million kw, and provides power for many of the factories and steel mills that line the river at this point. The city of Volgograd spreads along the right (western) bank of the Volga for nearly 80 km (50 miles).

Volgograd has a special place in the hearts of millions of Russians. This affection is symbolized by

the gigantic monument which looms above the city on Mamai Hill: a statue of Mother Russia carrying a drawn sword in her hand. Until 1961 the city was known as Stalingrad in honour of Josef Stalin, dictator of the Soviet Union for thirty years after the death of Lenin. During this period it was the scene of one of the most important battles of the Second World War, for in 1942 a prolonged siege of the city resulted in the greatest defeat ever suffered by the German army. At the end of the battle Stalingrad was saved, but it lay in ruins.

The rebuilding of the city was carefully planned to

Above   *The dam at Volgograd*

Below   *Stalin* (**right**) *with Lenin* (**left**) *in 1922*

Above *After the Second World War, Volgograd was completely rebuilt*

Below *The tree-lined shores of the Volga here make splendid beaches*

preserve and improve the natural environment. Today it is a garden city with avenues, parks and playgrounds, and stately public buildings. Some parks are located on low islands out in the stream, bordered with broad beaches which are popular spots for swimming and picnicking.

To the south of the city of Volgograd lies its busy port, and the entrance to the Volga-Don canal. Again, it was Peter the Great who first dreamed of a canal linking the Volga and Don rivers. Exploring the area early in the eighteenth century, he found that the Don river flowed roughly parallel to the Volga and only about 72 km (45 miles) away, in a direct line. But the land along that line was rocky and hilly, and the project of digging a canal there was too much for the engineering skills of the day. The resources of Peter's treasury were also inadequate, and the canal was still little more than a dream when he died in 1725.

In 1929, under the ambitious young Soviet regime, plans were again drawn up for a Volga-Don canal. But it was not until after the Second World War that work commenced. A new site was chosen, some distance south of the one selected by Peter the Great. This location meant that the rugged Volga Heights had to be crossed, and many engineers shook their heads at the challenge. But spurred on by the steel-willed Stalin, the work proceeded.

First the Don river was dammed, creating a large lake on the Heights. Canals were built at both ends of the lake: along one canal, locks would lift shipping from the low-lying Volga up to the lake, and along the other locks would lower vessels down the western

The Volga-Don canal linked the Volga with the busy centre of Rostov on the Don river

slope to the Don. By 1952 the work was complete, with 100 km (63 miles) of canals and 13 locks. Now some of the Volga traffic could continue down the Don to the Azov or Black Sea.

Most of the traffic leaving the Volga here is shifted to railway cars or even aeroplanes at Rostov-on-Don. Rostov is a busy industrial city as well as a transport centre, and is the gateway to the teeming factory and mining region of the Don basin. People of its new towns and cities are eager to buy farm goods from the sandy soil of the Volga delta.

To the Caspian through two hundred mouths

By the time the Volga reaches Volgograd, its surface is below the level of the world's great seas. But it continues to flow gently downstream across large areas of flat, semi-desert grass and scrubland. Its goal is the Caspian Sea, which lies 28 m (80 feet) below sea level.

Below Volgograd the river banks are flat, and the land generally featureless. Part of the river breaks off into a channel known as the Akhtuba; and countless lesser channels — many of them unnamed — wind and intertwine, separated by small, shifting islands.

As boats chug downstream between reedy banks, clouds of birds flash up with a loud whirring of wings. The Volga delta is on one of the world's greatest passages for migrating birds, and each year millions of birds pause among the narrow streamlets and grassy islands. A large area has been set aside as a nature reserve to protect the birds from hunters.

Fifty years ago, hunting birds for their brightly coloured feathers provided an important source of income for people who lived around the delta.

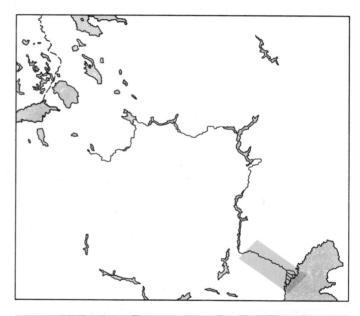

The sandpiper (right) and the giant pelican (far right) are just two of the 240 species of migrating birds which assemble in the delta each year

Above   *The port of Astrakhan lies at the head of the delta*

Left   *A carpet fair in old Astrakhan*

Today most of the villagers catch fish for a living. Some raise wine grapes in old vineyards, and others tend plots of melons, vegetables or grain. Many of their crops are shipped to market from the capital of the region, Astrakhan.

Astrakhan is one of the principal Caspian ports, although the city is not actually on the seashore — it lies far inland, at the head of the Volga delta. To a traveller approaching by water, the city appears as a sprawl of pale buildings, dusty and desert-hot in summer. In winter raw winds blow across the delta, and the river is frozen for about three months of the year.

Fortunately a railway from the north passes through Astrakahn on its way to the Caucasus. Trains bound for markets there carry delta-grown melons, wine, garden produce and grain, as well as

Above *Fishermen on the shore of the Caspian*

Left *Cotton from central Asia is one of the many goods which pass through Astrakhan on their way to distant markets*

fish and caviare. Oil from Baku, cotton from Turkestan, and timber from the mountains of the Caucasus all pass through Astrakhan by water or rail. And some aeroplanes land at the dusty airport nearby.

Astrakhan has known more prosperous days. Fishing and seal hunting used to be very lively industries. As soon as the ice broke in mid-March, vast shoals of fish — trout, pike, bream, perch, herring and sturgeon — rushed upstream to spawn. As recently as seventy years ago, 180,000 tons of fish were considered an average annual catch. About 40,000 young bachelor seals were killed in their breeding grounds in the northern Caspian.

These industries have dwindled in recent years. The level of the Caspian Sea has been dropping as a result of the use of water upstream for irrigation, industry and hydro-electric plants. There is also a great loss from surface evaporation; and other causes, less well understood, may also contribute to the steadily dropping level. This has caused silt to block many of the channels up which fish used to swim in spring, to spawn. This has been particularly hard on the giant Caspian sturgeon — the sole producer of the black-gold caviare for which Russia is famous. The government, concerned about this valuable crop, has started fish hatcheries upstream

Below *Caviare consists of the pressed and salted eggs of the sturgeon*

Above *The giant Caspian sturgeon often grows to lengths of 3 m (9¾ feet) or more*

Right *The oilfields at Baku on the Caspian have proved to be a major source of pollution*

on the Volga. Millions of young fish are released into the river each year, and as a result the catch has shown some improvement.

Another serious problem is pollution in the waters of the Volga and Caspian. Wastes from the industrial cities upstream on the Volga have flowed into the delta and on into the great inland lake. The oil fields of Baku, farther south on the Caspian, also contribute. This pollution has had a ruinous effect on

Today's caravans still look much as they did on the old Silk Road

the small fish and crustaceans that used to form the diet of the sturgeon and other large fish, as well as of the seals. With the dwindling of the fish population, real Russian caviare has become a costly luxury indeed.

The Soviet government has ordered cities and industries to treat sewage and factory wastes so that they will not damage the river and its wildlife. But Astrakhan's fisheries and rookeries have not yet wholly recovered.

The city of Astrakhan was once a proud capital of the Tatar khans. Its buildings were mainly low mud-brick structures, tightly clustered along narrow lanes, around them a sea of the snug, round Tatar tents called *yurts* or *girs*, fashioned of golden-yellow wool felt. Camel caravans, stretching as far as the eye could see, plodded towards the city. And in the courtyards of the merchant inns, also called *khans*, a wealth of colourful silks, spices and other exotic goods were unloaded. So many pelts of silky, tightly curled Persian lamb made their way into Russian markets through this city that the fur came to be known as 'astrakhan'.

Even in those long-ago days, the prosperity of Astrakhan depended on trade up and down the Volga. And then, as today, Russia's greatest river flowed sluggishly past the sun-baked city to empty into an inland sea through two hundred shallow mouths.

Right *This wall decoration at Baku recalls the role of the Caspian ports in trade between the East and the West*

Glossary

Basin The area of countryside drained by a river and its tributaries.

Burlaki 'The Volga boatmen', men and women who hauled loaded barges up the river in old Russia.

City-state An independent state consisting of a city and the countryside around it.

Cossacks Horsemen of southern Russia in the time of the tsars.

Dam A barrier built across a stream to hold back the flow of water.

Delta A flat plain built up around a river's mouth by the stream laying deposits of silt.

Hydro-electric plant A power plant in which electricity is generated by using the energy of flowing or falling water.

Hydrofoil A vessel with wing-like fittings that lift the hull above the water when the boat reaches a certain speed.

Kolkhoz A collective farm on which workers share in the profits.

Kremlin The citadel or fortress of a Russian city. 'The Kremlin' refers to the citadel of Moscow, seat of the central government of the USSR.

Lock A chamber in a canal, with gates that can be opened and closed to change the water level and thus raise or lower ships.

Mongols Pastoral nomads from Mongolia who, in the twelfth and thirteenth centuries, formed fierce armies and conquered a vast empire including much of Asia and Russia.

Muscovy The kingdom (grand duchy) based in Moscow, which expanded its power to form the Russian Empire.

Pollution The contamination of soil, air or water.

Principality A small state ruled by a prince.

Serf A servant bound to the land and required to work for its owner.

Silk Road One of several overland trade routes linking the Orient and Europe in ancient and mediaeval times.

Soviet A council of elected members, with governmental powers.

Sovkhoz A State-owned farm on which workers are paid wages.

Steppe A vast, treeless grassland.

Taiga Coniferous evergreen forests found in sub-arctic lands.

Tatar A member of 'the Golden Horde' of Genghis Khan, one of the Mongolian tribes that overran much of Asia and Russia in the Middle Ages.

Trans-ship To transfer goods from one boat or ship to another.

Tributary A stream which joins a larger river system.

Vikings Seafaring raiders from Scandinavia in about the eighth to the tenth centuries. Known in Russia as the Varangians.

Facts and figures

Length of Volga river: 3,680 km (nearly 2,300 miles).
Area of Volga basin: 1,442,050 sq km (563,300 sq miles).
Population of Volga basin: more than 70 million people.
Navigable waterways of Volga system: 32,000 km (20,000 miles), including about 200 tributaries.
Widest section of the Volga: 50 km (30 miles) at the junction with the Kama river in the Kuibyshev reservoir.
Major dams and power plants: Gorodets, 400,000 kw; Kuibyshev, 2,300,000 kw; Rybinsk, 830,000 kw; Volgograd, 2,560,000 kw.
Length of major canals: Moscow-Volga canal, 128 km (80 miles); Volga-Baltic waterway (Mariinsk system), 1,128 km (701 miles); Volga-Don canal, 101 km (63 miles).

Some important dates

c. 900 Scandinavian chieftains establish themselves in northern Russia amongst Finnish tribes settled along the upper Volga.
c. 1000-1200 Slavic tribes move into mid-Volga region.
1239-1242 Mongol invaders conquer much of Russia.
1552 Kazan, capital of Tatars, taken. Ivan IV, prince of Muscovy, declares himself tsar of all the Russias.
1712 Tsar Peter builds the first Baltic-Volga canal.
1810 Baltic-Volga canal expanded to the Mariinsk system.
1917 Russian Revolution.
1937 Moscow-Volga canal completed.
1952 Volga-Don canal completed, linking the Volga with the Azov, Black and Mediterranean seas.
1957 Kuibyshev and Gorodets dams completed.

Further reading

Cole, J. P. *Geography of the USSR* (Pelican, 1967)

Dewdney, J. C. *Geography of the Soviet Union* (Pergamon Press, 1971)

Grey, Ian *History of Russia* (Horizon, 1970)

Hall, Elvajean *Volga: Life Line of Russia* (E. M. Hale & Co., 1965)

McGraw Hill *Encyclopaedia of Russia and the Soviet Union* (1961)

Parker, W. H. *The Russians* (David & Charles, 1973; Praeger Publishers, 1973)

St George, George *Russia* (Batsford, 1973)

Sochurek, H. 'The Volga, Russia's Mighty River Road' *(National Geographic Magazine,* May 1973)

Van der Post, Laurens *Journey into Russia* (Hogarth Press, 1964; as *A View of All the Russias,* William Morrow & Co., 1964)

Wallace, Robert *Rise of Russia* (Silver Burdett Company)

Watson, Jane Werner *The Volga, Russia's River of the Five Seas* (Garrard, 1973)

ACKNOWLEDGEMENTS

T. W. Calloway: 51; Stephen Durnien: 41 bottom, 47, 49 top, 50 bottom; Wilson Forbes: 9 top, 27; Eric Hosking: 9 bottom, 16 top left, 52; Mansell Collection: 10 top; John Massey Stewart: 17, 18, 24, 25 top, 28, 29 top, 37 top, 42, 48 top, 54; Novosti: *cover,* 6, 13, 14, 25 bottom, 30, 39, 40 top right, 43, 44, 45, 50 top, 53, 55, 58; John Summers: 41 top, 48 bottom; John Topham Picture Library: 31 bottom; Jane Werner Watson: *frontispiece,* 7, 12, 15, 16 top right, 20, 21, 23, 31 top, 32, 33, 34, 35, 36 bottom, 56, 57, 59, 60, 61. Drawings and photographs on pages 8, 10 bottom, 11, 16 bottom, 19, 22, 26, 29 bottom, 36 top, 37 bottom, 40 left, 46, and 49 bottom are from the Wayland Picture Library. Maps by the Hayward Art Group.

Index

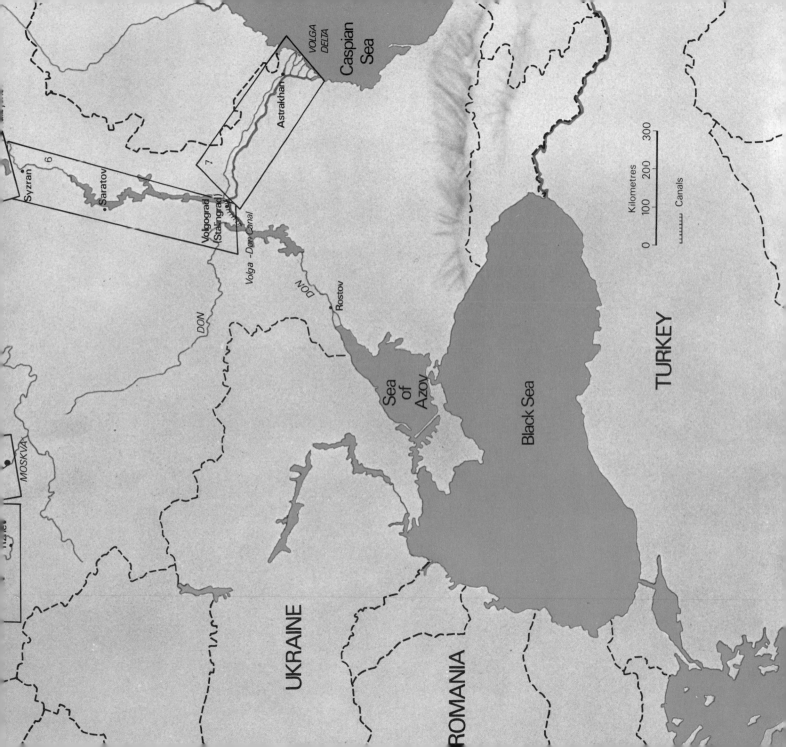

VOLGA DELTA

Caspian Sea

Astrakhan

7

6

Syzran

Saratov

Volgograd (Stalingrad)

Volga - Don Canal

DON

DON

Rostov

MOSKVA

Sea of Azov

Black Sea

UKRAINE

ROMANIA

TURKEY

Kilometres

300

200

100

0

Canals

44484

947
WAT

Watson, Jane Werner.

The Volga.

ALBUQUERQUE ACADEMY MID SCHOOL